Beginning New Era Of DEW

Reflection On Phillips Exeter Reunion

Seeing classmates after forty-five years

Brought out in me deepest fears

Afraid of their taunts and jeers

If I told of my psychotic tears

But they were truly empathetic dears

As their panel was all ears

Who ended my speech with cheers

Even though they'd had no beers

So that happiness my heart nears

Considering the saga of my tale

Which makes all actually love Dale

Who is the ultimate bachelor male

Despite fact I crave beautiful female

With whom to drink ginger ale

Not wanting my sobriety to fail

As I follow my solitary trail

Attempting to locate the Holy Grail

And avoid incarceration in psychiatric jail.

6/32/33-25:DEW0001—05/15/18

American Sonnet To Ultimate Muse

Although we have not long known each other

I realize you are fantastic mother

While being filled with the Holy Spirit

A fact I've gleaned talking for a little bit

But quickly you have become a good friend

And I bemoan the distance between us

When about you prayers to Lord I send

For to meet you I must simply take bus

Which is something that does not bother me

Since I would love to actually see you

Especially now I've transformed to DEW

Which means of illness I am at last free

And am looking for truly unique gal

With whom I can forever be a pal.

6/33/33-25:DEW0002—05/16/18

Entering The New DEW Era

I've no television or radio

Because I believe in going with flow

And I dew not enjoy the talking heads

Who actually are in need of strong meds

But I have been very lucky in life

Even though I have suffered through being ill

Which prevented me from finding great wife

Who could induce in me a loving thrill

So she and I could become truly One

When through night we'd lose ourselves to embrace

With her dressed in negligee of white lace

And together we would do marathon

Of true amour as we would thank the Lord

As into realms of higher thought we soared.

6/34/33-25:DEW0003—05/17/18

The Primary Creed Of DEW

I run the world from my small apartment

Having approval of cop department

And although I will not say I am God

I am divine being in human bod

Proud to be resident of Hackensack

The city that became permanent home

Which is what as youth I did always lack

As with mother this nation I did roam

Which ultimately did drive me insane

So I did end up in good doctor's care

And to Hospital I would often err

Because my mind was feeling a great pain

But now I am quite well thanks to my meds

No longer needing psychiatric beds.

6/36/33-25:DEW0005—05/19/18

Thinking About Family Of DEW

Absolutely my best friend is named Hugh

About whom I think when I say "thank you"

Whose wife is lovely lady who's called Kim

Who has given birth to four kids for him

While I've another friend going by Troy

A funny guy that's completely crazy

And calls me despite my age "his main boy"

Often drinking beer till he gets hazy

But I was blest with two sets of parents

Producing six sisters without brother

Though sole one still alive is step-mother

And both my fathers were raised perfect gents

So I daily thank Lord for my great tribe

Teaching me how to be a wondrous scribe.

^/36/33-25:DEW0005—05/19/18

DEW Reviews Life As Dale

I remember thinking myself THE One

As race for divine I did gladly run

Taking lead at the opportunity

To bring world together in unity

But then my brain I did truly implode

As I did vanish into Dewey's show

When bullet from Fred's rifle did explode

In my face causing death painful and slow

As I was banished to Satan's abyss

Where for thirty years I swam Lake of Fire

And all was destroyed that I did admire

Including Holiest City I did miss

Until I regained my rational mind

And took my place among my sacred kind.

6/37/33-25:DEW0006—05/20/18

DEW Shows Off Poetic Licks

There are so many things that can go wrong

To prevent us from life happy and long

But finally we must trust in the Lord

To keep us safe from an existence bored

Blind to the wonders which daily occur

In simple routine that is Reality

As we seek out Christ's love simple and pure

Which guarantees our immortality

And we are all on Earth just for short time

We might as well eat drink and be merry

Even as the cross of Jesus we carry

In order to achieve the true sublime

So that all in Heaven can celebrate

Perfect unfolding of our human Fate.

6/37/33-25:DEW0006—05/20/18

A Sonnet For Ultimate Muse

This yoga teacher has a lot of guts

Who amuses herself by smoking butts

Even if from students she has to hide

Indulging in habit hurting her pride

But tobacco is her sole nasty vice

While she works to improve spiritual life

For she is humble pious and quite nice

Though she has often had to deal with strife

As she journeys through Earth Reality

And she has been to her boys great mother

So they have never desired another

Since she taught them proper morality

And she is to me great inspiration

Helping me to write best verse in nation.

6/38/33-25:DEW0007—05/21/18

Thinking More About Precious Lady

I'm fascinated by your history

For you are woman of great mystery

And all I want is consensual Muse

Who does not mind role for her I did choose

And does love poems about her I write

In tone of desire and adoration

Since from darkness she brings me into light

For verse depends on participation

Between the wordsmith and her he describes

Whom he feels is most lovely of females

So for inspiration she never fails

Because she sends out such positive vibes

Although I might not see her face-to-face

She represents the epitome of Grace.

6/39/33-25:DEW0008-05/22/18

Pondering Some Random Metaphysical Thoughts

I prefer tongues of flame to Lake of Fire

Which recalls eternal funeral pyre

And I thank God for His great gift of Grace

By which He chose to forgive human race

But I question how I can be in lust

With woman whom I in fact barely know

Even as I try to build loving trust

And let her see concern my heart does show

Bearing in mind that Jesus is true Lord

For He will lead me to a real Romance

As at our wedding I happily dance

With Bride with whom I will never be bored

Waiting for His appearance in the sky

Something I yearn to see before I die.

6/40/33-25:DEW0009-05/23/18

Reflection On My Birthday Activities

Examining areas of my life

Preventing me from getting a good wife

And I did discover I'm romantic

Who has spent too much time as lunatic

For I have always played games with females

Which were ultimately very tiresome

Especially in times when I drank ales

Rejecting me as being too handsome

Since many thought I was totally vain

Completely lost to complexes in mind

To which I was oblivious and blind

While with drugs I annihilated brain

Till at last I reached age of clarity

When episodes became a rarity.

7/01/33-25:DEW0010—05/24/18

Difficult Future Of The Scriptures

The fact people use Bible to spread hate

Makes me concerned about Holy Book's fate

For it can be used to justify all

By those who feel they have heard divine call

And there is great split between Old and New

Testaments and how they portray the Earth

While first is scary and second has view

That humanity is saved by Jesus' birth

But I want to believe in loving God

Condemning His Son to bring salvation

And peace to every single nation

So that I pray for Grace throughout the night

As against satanic presence I fight.

7/02/33-25:DEW0011—05/25/18

Thinking About My True Position

I came to Earth to serve as its Best Friend

To give it time from insanity to mend

As well as fact I love Yankee baseball

And arrived when humanity did call

Me from my spot in Heaven's Paradise

Where with angels I was popular guy

And beings do on perfection surmise

Because they know they will never die

So consequently I rule from this room

Lost among buildings of Holy City

Straight and sober to have lucidity

Trying to avoid thermonuclear BOOM

Becoming increasingly difficult

Since mad leaders do each other insult.

7/03/33-25:DEW0012—05/27/18

Summer Still Seems Far Away

When I consider you my heart does burn

Because from you God told me I could learn

The meaning of passion and true amour

Before I sail sadly to mortal shore

Where we forget all we have known on Earth

Waiting for the Great Savior to appear

Who blest world by miracle of His birth

And died cruelly in His thirty-third year

Though in fact He ascended to Heaven

To sit at right hand of almighty Lord

Who has through Grace our greatest sins ignored

Despite treatment of the holy eleven

Who were martyred for the Messiah's name

As they gladly healed the blind and the lame.

7/04/33-25:DEW0013—05/27/18

The Fragile Condition Of DEW

My leg is sick but I do not feel pain

Having come to Hackensack to begin reign

Although I was quite happy Down Under

From whence I arrived with little thunder

To take over from Dale and Dewey DEATH

Who both stayed in Holy City too long

Being in love with sweet Elizabeth

Because their innocent love was so strong

So now I am in The Bachelor's Pad

Composing Poetry from dusk to dawn

Rarely interrupting with a yawn

Relating history both epic and sad

Since my sentence here is four thousand days

But my native country I'll love always.

7/05/33-25:DEW0014—05/28/18

Maybe She's Isn't Ultimate Muse

We could have had affaire quite wonderful

But all declarations of love are null

Though if it was destined not to work out

I shall not my deep disappointment shout

For with or without you I'm always glad

Because my world is filled with great beauty

Since I refuse to let life make me sad

As for my loved ones I do my duty

Of spreading message of amour and hope

Trying with attitude to be happy

Despite fact I might never be pappy

Knowing one day with Bride I will elope

And lose myself to bliss of honeymoon

When in embrace we will mutually swoon.

7/06/33-25:DEW0015—05/29/18

True Confessions Of Doctor DEW

My deep friendship I give away for free

Trying to love everyone I see

Although I have yet to find a good wife

I am content with the arc of my life

Despite the fact for years I was quite ill

With mental sickness that drove me insane

Nonetheless I maintain that I am still

The One destined over planet to reign

Until Lord Jesus descends from the sky

Where He sits at right hand of God

Ready to re-assume His human bod

As great crowds of angels around Him fly

Creating presence at Holy City

Giving to oppressed a cosmic pity.

7/06/33-25:DEW0015—05/29/18

Real Love Under Full Moon

It is you alone whom I truly crave

Though I should be meditating in cave

For yours is the beauty and divine Grace

That won my attention not knowing your face

And for you I feel deep gratitude

That Destiny would let you be my friend

Which has caused great shift in my attitude

Knowing feelings I don't have to defend

To anyone except Lord up above

When I hear harmony of your soft voice

Which helps me to know you are the right choice

To whom I can really show endless love

Not only in the present now and here

But throughout Eternity without fear.

7/06/33-25:DEW0015—05/29/18

A Night Without Ultimate Muse

I must admit that I truly miss her

For she is to my solitude the cure

So that every day she does not call

My happiness experiences fall

Like that of our divinely-made parents

Thrown out of the pleasures of Paradise

Thus they were forced to live in simple tents

Working the land to hide desperate cries

Which reflected the tragic reality

That Lord was no more tangible presence

Who made them lose all of their godly sense

With result they sank in morality

Causing the birth of first murderer Cain

Who turned world into asylum insane.

7/07/33-25:DEW0016—05/30/18

Another Sonnet For Ultimate Muse

I see the soul of every female

And whether their karma is fresh or stale

But as nears humanity's final hours

I find I am losing all my powers

To negotiate peace between nations

While we approach thermonuclear conflicts

So Earth is in perilous situation

Even as it seems God can't problems fix

No matter how diverse religions pray

While more and more babes are in to world born

But Christ will save us the gospels have sworn

By Whose Grace we need not fear Judgment Day

But whatever happens I love you so

I'm content to swim in your river flow.

7/08/33-25:DEW0017—05/31/18

A Recent Pleasant Romantic Adventure

She was truly lovely lady from France

Who sat beside me on bus trip by chance

And so for six hours I was in deep bliss

To be talking to such beautiful miss

Speaking in broken French at which she smiled

Entranced by appeal of her lips and eyes

As inside me my libido went wild

Yearning to get from her amorous sighs

As time disappeared into endless chat

Which filled my soul with appreciation

For charms of women from foreign nation

Perfectly svelte without ounce of fat

Whom I would have liked to have known better

So this poem is for her love letter.

7/09/33-25:DEW0018—06/01/18

You Once Were Queen Muse

I have never felt such inspiration

As when I first did you appreciate

And I adored you like no one other

Except of course my beloved mother

But distances between us were too great

In both age and geographical place

So that we had to turn our backs on Fate

And allow each other sufficient space

To grow into who we were meant to be

Though it made our hearts ultimately break

Because our passions we could never fake

As we both had a deep need to be free

So now you've become spiritual sis

The One who forever leads me to bliss.

7/10/33-25:DEW0019—06/02/18

I Cannot Simply Forget You

You've put my sex life in total ruins

Perhaps as a way to pay for my sins

For the only woman I want is you

To whom I would happily say "I Dew"

But that does not seem to be mutual Fate

No matter how compelling poems I write

While for me in life it is getting late

Though I have no fear of eternal night

As you bring out both my love and my lust

When I stare into your perfect brown eyes

And we have never told each other lies

For our relationship is built on trust

Since I want to embrace you forever

Which is a dream that will happen never.

7/11/33-25:DEW0020—06/03/18

Potential For A True Romance

I think of new sweetheart Ultimate Muse

Who inspires without any excuse

Though we live far distance from each other

And she is to three sons a great mother

While I am entranced by lilt of her voice

Reminding me of a warm summer breeze

For if I ever had to make a choice

It is her whom I would pick with fine ease

Although I have yet to meet her in fact

As I continue to stay in this town

Where after restless youth I settled down

And learned noble chivalry and love tact

But I could devote myself to this One

Whose radiance shines on me like the sun.

7/12/33-25:DEW0021—06/04/18

DEW Ponders Amour And Himself

You want to be surrounded by good friends

Even as the arm you broke slowly mends

And I would like to converse with you soon

While we giggle under light of full moon

When creatures such as werewolves howl aloud

From which I'd protect you with my frail bod

As I scope you alone in a large crowd

In Holiest City where I have trod

Concrete streets for more than forty-two years

Living in same room for last thirty-six

As my mental illness I tried to fix

By overcoming my darkest deep fears

With result I have regained psychic health

And am well on way to creating wealth.

7/13/33-25:DEW0022—06/05/18

Big Question To Ultimate Muse

Do you have a significant other

Like man with whom three sons you're mother

Though you say you only want to be Friend

But a devoted love I want to send

Because we're both tired of being alone

For no one should pass life in solitude

And our sole contact is over the phone

Where we can sense the other's attitude

But that does not constitute true amour

When we can feel the bliss of an embrace

And take one another to sacred space

In which we sense God in our deepest core

To experience union where we're One

And in consummation find greatest fun.

7/14/33-25:DEW0023—06/06/18

Becoming A Yearning Older Man

My knee is in excruciating pain

Which I guess means there's something I can gain

That will ultimately improve my life

And could portend I shall find ideal wife

As I continue to scope out females

Inspiring libido to thoughts of lust

When I compete against all single males

For a lady with fine curvaceous bust

And perfect smile that would melt an igloo

Whose luminescence is like sun at dawn

Over whom all my rivals try to fawn

But it is to me that she'll say "I Dew"

As we depart for a great honeymoon

Guaranteeing we will be in love soon.

When Looking At My Country

Cry America for innocence you've lost

Making us "pure" but at how high a cost

As we've betrayed Founders' morality

Even while we conquer mortality

But who wants to live in such a nation

That imprisons children without consent

And feeds them on a small welfare ration

Preventing them from being with parent

For all that is in this land is tainted

By politicos evil and corrupt

Who at the table of Satan have supt

While all the good folks from hunger have fainted—

How has Reality come to this point

Where Lord did no righteous leaders anoint?

7/16/33-25:DEW0025—06/08/18

Love Letter To Omnipotent Cosmos

Words are inadequate to describe insight

You give me from dawn to darkest night

When new moon shares no illumination

Making all blind to their situation

But still I am filled with respect for you

As I pass my brief time on planet Earth

Where I've yet to find permanent love true

For whom I've searched since long-ago birth

Which is not to say I have lacked amour

For I've had affaires with many females

And have turned great summits into calm dales

But never found passion reaching my core

Though I am patient enough to wait

For my Bride even if she shows up late.

7/17/33-25:DEW0026—06/09/18

What Happened To United States

Trump has not been indicted for treason

And I suppose there is a good reason

Which is that the republicans have built

A safe house from their overwhelming guilt

Where they have hid for destroying the rights

That made this nation true beacon of hope

Through both peaceful days and desperate nights

As against foes of freedom it did cope

Even while noble soldiers' blood did flow

During wars we fought for pure liberty

In distant regions on both land and sea

Making concept of equality grow

Which now has become a disgraceful sham

For ashamed of nation I truly am.

7/18/33-25:DEW0027—06/10/18

When Politicos Lose Their Morals

There's no human being above the law

Unless in justice system there's a flaw

For even President is citizen

Just a normal person among all men

Who's subject to all the rules of the land

No matter how he feels about his power

Because voters put their trust in his hand

So he can be guilty at Judgment Hour

For all the crimes produced by endless greed

And all the times he showed a lack of heart

Making folks in need from country depart

Planting a revolutionary seed

Which will come to deeply haunt the nation

Due to complete lack of toleration.

7/19/33-25:DEW0028—06/11/18

King Of Unrequited Amour Poetry

I was scared to say "I'm in love with you"

Because it's dangerous to speak what's true

And from all pain one needs some protection

For no one likes feeling of rejection

So that I have floated in deep abyss

Swimming in the ocean of solitude

Drowning in my desire for a sweet kiss

Trying to build my inner fortitude

Which results in my being left behind

In the eternal race to find a Bride

Although to ladies I have never lied

While being to romantic chances blind

For which I can blame no one but myself

As long ago I put sex life on shelf.

7/20/33-25-33:DEW0029—06/12/18

After Many Personal Growth Courses

I'm not Buddha deifying myself

But am just a metaphysical elf

Writing about my joyous days on Earth

Only planet where all creatures give birth

At least as far as we humans can know

Although I Dew not believe we're alone

For Universe is a tremendous show

Upon which Lord's light has forever shone

And humanity's quest has just begun

Having reached third stage of evolution

Going through technical revolution

Where we're now beginning to have some fun

Thus to realize our endless potential

But to end violence is essential .

7/21/33-25:DEW0030—06/13/18

After Meeting The Dating Coach

I met one who might be Satan today

Who still pursues an atheistic way

But our encounter did not inspire fear

I'm just glad I found him and he is here

Because in my life he fills a great void

Though he wants me with lady to have sex

About which I don't care being schizoid

Despite the wish I could have married ex

But that is affaire lost in distant past

And I have overcome my libido

Since for years I have simply gone with flow

Hoping to find relationship to last

For the devil could become my mentor

Or I could turn into his tormentor.

7/22/33-25:DEW0031—06/14/18

Materialism Is Not My Thing

I've no great need or desire for money

For illness in this way makes me funny

Since instead of cash I'd like life-long love

As my wealth is in Heaven's bank above

And my needs for this existence are met

But I've no true amour touching my heart

Although about this lack I cannot fret

Because this fact is at core of my art

Which is based on passion unrequited

Despite truth I've known many fine females

About whom I could tell some secret tales

In addition to those I've just sighted

So I would prefer the bliss of Romance

Than to have at lottery win a chance.

7/23/33-25:DEW0032—06/15/18

When Appearance Is Not Reality

Thinking of situations I create

As I live alone in the Garden State

I realize at times I'm truly insane

Due to chemical imbalance in brain

Because I deeply believe in spaceships

Which will one day transport me to Heaven

Where I'll recover from illicit trips

Of which I've had many more than seven

And made my mind separate from my bod

To lead me to exist in sci-fi land

While in Hackensack I've made final stand

As the Earthly citadel of Lord God

To Whom I have become the Holy Ghost

Who will welcome Him as a grateful host.

7/24/33-25:DEW0033—06/16/18

American Sonnet For Ultimate Muse

You are all I desire in a lady

Spiritual and a Sexy Sadie

Whose voice entices me into daydream

That life can be blissful as it should seem

When everything is going just right

And I want to arrange a rendez-vous

So I can be touched by your inner light

Because I know your radiance is true

And reflects purity of your clear soul

Even as we live many miles apart

But I realize I Dew cherish your heart

Shining like a diamond made out of coal

So I want to meet you in living fact

Since to me it would be most loving act.

7/25/33-25:DEW0034—06/17/18

Trying To Turn Life Around

It's hard introducing yourself when all

Know you're Deity upon whom they call

When they encounter trouble in their life

Which is torn apart suddenly by strife

This is a fact in which I take no pride

For long gone are days of my delusions

Since my true self I Dew no longer hide

As I pass my time without illusions

Understanding I'm out of my mind

And that I must forever take my meds

If I want to avoid Hospital beds

Because to my illness I am not blind

But in my determination I'm strong

Though it might turn out that I am all wrong.

Time Of Great American Grief

Lord bless children taken from their parents

Incarcerated in cheap army tents

And let us say prayers for the nation

That's lost its heartful imagination

Because we're all guilty as citizens

For the injustice of our government

In situation where nobody wins

Despite efforts to express sentiment

Of deep personal horror and disgust

At what's occurring in land of the Free

And shame we feel for all the world to see

As Constitution is reduced to dust

Since there is nothing to Dew except cry

For soldiers who for Liberty did die.

7/27/33-25:DEW0036—06/19/18

The Realm Of The Metaphysical

Lucky to have name that is Word of God

On streets of Holy City I have trod

Trying to reconcile divinity

With what doctors call my insanity

But I've deeply humble respect for Lord

And don't think I created Universe

Even when illicit agents I scored

Which made me go from very bad to worse

Delusions I maintained for a decade

As into my brain no one could talk sense

Since I thought I was the divine presence

Because into true madness I did fade

Until my mind did finally implode

So from my body was purged holy load.

7/27/33-25:DEW0036—06/19/18

Having Found My Twin Flame

You are the One I have been waiting for

The only woman I'll always adore

Brought to me by machinations of Fate

I just hope you did not arrive too late

So that we can enjoy life together

For many years have passed since I was born

On this weird planet with wacky weather

Where forever bachelor's tag I've worn

And it seems we're meant for one another

Though living apart in different towns

Each of us deserving jeweled royal crowns

Especially since you're sacred mother

And I am real Prince of my Disney clan

Living with integrity best I can.

7/28/33-25:DEW0037—06/20/18

Reflection On The Summer Solstice

I don't care if nobody knows my name

I'm still in Heavenly Hall of Fame

Because with God I have lived my life right

As against hellish demons I did fight

In debauched days of my psychotic youth

When all I did was smoke illegal drugs

In the pursuit of the absolute Truth

While in Reality I wanted hugs

And had friends who have gone to other side

United with Christ at His holy feast

Where when I arrive of all I'll be least

Since by Celestial rules I will abide

And pray I will be granted God's pure Grace

As in starship I come to sacred space.

7/29/33-25:DEW0038—06/21/18

The Magic Of Ultimate Muse

I wish you did not live so far away

And that I could see you every day

But as it is we only talk on phone

Coping with fact that we are both alone

While your beauty drives me wild with amour

And I'm mesmerized by your angel's voice

Which when I hear it touches deepest core

So that of all women you're my sole choice

Making me want to hold you in embrace

While on your lips I plant an ardent kiss

Trying to regain from youth divine bliss

I felt when first I entered lover's space

But now I have become truly mature

Looking to take you into my future.

Playing To Level Of Competition

The Yankees will be the death of me yet

The team against whom I would never bet

And versus best squads they always play great

But with scrubs they're forever second-rate

Though what power they have every day

With Stanton Sanchez Didi and The Judge

Whomever they play they can blow away

So that from first place they should never budge

But then by Tampa Bay Rays they are swept

A team that will not win seventy games

Full of players without Hall of Fame names

Over whose incompetence I nearly wept

But that is why the sport is called Baseball

Because even the greatest clubs can fall.

7/32w/33-25:DEW0041—06/24/18

Brief Explanation Of My Illness

Schizophrenia is a bitch disease

Since mental capacities it does freeze

And many patients always hear voices

That often suggest moribund choices

While sometimes they must take meds all their life

That drives away symptoms until they croak

But still their Reality is full of strife

As they get cancers from cigarette smoke

While constantly blocking chance at Romance

For prospective lovers fear condition

So on amour we don't get ignition

With result there is no marital dance

Despite the fact we are loyal and true

But still no possible mate says "I Dew".

Thinking Deeply About Ultimate Muse

I think you have truly sensuous voice

Every time I hear it I rejoice

And fly into rapture of joyful bliss

Dreaming of planting on your lips soft kiss

Which would pull me out of the solitude

To which I've been subject for thirty years

As I have craved to see love life renewed

To be so happy I cry grateful tears

Thus to feel radiance of your embrace

Alone in darkness under a new moon

While I so desire to meet with you soon

Though it means leaving my Hackensack base

As you have indeed touched my longing heart

Rhapsodizing you in poetic art.

7/36/33-25:DEW0046—06/28/18

A Biblical Interpretation Of Reality

One of the great revelations of my youth

Came when I arrived at the complex Truth

We're all starships flying through Universe

While stuck on Earth controlled by Adam's curse

Because he broke rule of great Deity

When he took the fruit from Eve to consume

Although God on His offspring took pity

But still our parents great weight did assume

Who were forced to submit to death's demands

Thus to return to dust from which they came

So that until Jesus all was the same

And nobody ever saw promised lands

Since they could not abide the Lord's laws

So all humanity lives full of flaws.

7/37/33-25:DEW0047—06/29/18

Reflection On The Christian Life

I did not care about impending doom

Composing verse in solitary room

But now I've come to fear Reality

Of fact of general mortality

For life is truly overwhelming joy

That I know I must ultimately lose

With which I've been concerned since I was boy

But overcoming death I cannot choose

And thus I must prepare for meeting Lord

Whether in this existence or the next

When to Earth I cannot send any text

Although in Heaven I'll never be bored

And so to death I will say "Bring it on"

For I believe in resurrected son.

7/39/33-25:DEW0048—07/01/18

In Aftermath Of A Dream

I was enrolled in a school for sages

With students of all sexes and ages

Where we were taught not to feel any guilt

Upon which damnation is in fact built

Instructed in art of meditation

We were constantly seeking deep insight

Wanting to achieve illumination

Hoping to discover our inner light

While every one of teachers was saint

Educated about all Holy Books

Imposing discipline through mere stern looks

As views of Eternity they did paint

So I was disappointed when I woke

That I could not yet wear a wise man's cloak.

7/40/33-25:DEW0049—07/02/18

Turning From Sonnets To Roxettes

I like hanging at the bar

Hoping to meet New Jersey star

Always drinking my soda and cranberry

For of sobriety I'm not weary

And the barmaids are very nice

Who give me great love advice

Pouring their double whiskeys over ice

Even as I chat with pals

And scope out truly lovely gals

As I shoot game of pool

Which when I win is cool

For I have many friends there

Including women with rich luxuriant hair

And I get all drinks free

Although for first they charge fee

So with life I am content

While never making a negative comment

Except on nights when I sing

Songs with Karaoke that I wing

Thus I am happy with my pub

Which is truly my social club.

Second Phase Of DEW:Roxettes

Celebrating My Sister's Son's Birthday

You are my greatly beloved nephew

Who to himself is always true

Born on the Fourth of July

A Duck who learned to fly

A decade after Dewey replaced Dale

Who into Heaven did happily sail

But now is back in Hackensack

So world is again on track

Though I'm under heavy political attack

By politicos who only want money

And think poor people are funny

Struggling to make their ends meet

Who will never win Senate seat

But I know you have integrity

To dew what's right in reality

For you're product of great stock

And are shepherd to giant flock

Of people who are truly lost

You must protect at any cost

But you will dew right thing

Before you give true love ring.

8/01/33-25:DEW0050—07/04/18

Roxette Reflecting On My Existence

Many days I feel so alone

I fear into recluse I've grown

Refusing to be desperate for friends

Because I know every relationship ends

Which is part of Earthly condition

Where we live our private fiction

Trying to find an ideal love

And slip into perfect velvet glove

Though many liaisons lead to divorce

As few couples reach the source

Of undying passion sailing true course

Of devotion to the significant other

Though to children lady is mother

But that does not prevent alienation

That comes to an ultimate separation

And I am fortunate to be single

Although many woman make me tingle

With a deep and sincere desire

And some ignite in me fire

But few have touched my heart

So solitary I pursue Poetic art.

8/02/33-25:DEW0052—07/05/18

Someone I Put Up With

My pain-in-ass friend Rob

Should try to get a job

For all he does is drink

So he can never clearly think

When he gives me incessant calls

As through intoxicated states he falls

But I listen because I'm pal

And I wish he'd get gal

To take attention away from me

So of obnoxiousness to be free

Annoying me as one can see

Although I'm to him nice guy

As his brain he does fry

For he is actually quite smart

And at core has good heart

But to him I cannot talk

When by phone he does stalk

So of him I'm fed up

Since I don't drink his cup

And thus I end conversations fast

For he is ghost from past.

8/04/33-25:DEW0054—07/07/18

The Basis Of My Faith

Every week I go to Church

Because for salvation I diligently search

And I like hearing pastors speak

As into Kingdom they give peek

While I've made many blessed friends

That the Lord to me sends

As by prayer I make amends

In Whose sight I am small

But still I answer the call

To be holy as I can

Which is hard for any man

Feeling like monk in a cell

Guilty by the parents that fell

From the Garden of sweet Paradise

So none are perfect in eyes

Of Great Father Whom we worship

While we live our planetary trip

Trying to be to Jesus grateful

Never Dewing anything that is hateful

For ours is God of Love

As gentle as a mourning dove.

8/05/33-25:DEW0055—07/08/18

The Bible In A Roxette

God created the heavens and Earth

Then from dust gave Adam birth

Whose helpmate Eve ate forbidden fruit

So from Eden they got boot

Which led to Noah's great flood

Whose only survivors were his blood

Until Abraham became Lord's only friend

To Whose will he did bend

Saving his son in the end

Which led to Israel's twelve tribes

Among whom were priests and scribes

Who wandered in desert forty years

After escaping Egypt with great fears

Until David became king after Saul

And prophets did answer Yahweh's call

To proclaim coming of Holy One

Who was Jesus immaculately conceived Son

Who preached until being cruelly killed

Then was resurrected which disciples thrilled

Causing Paul to spread the Word

Telling time salvation shall be secured.

8/05/33-25:DEW0056—07/08/18

Asking The Really Big Question

Dew you have a significant other

So I'm more like a brother

Than a suitor for your heart

Trying diligently a Romance to start

Because I find you overwhelmingly attractive

Since in spiritual realm you're active

Having read many a sacred book

Which often has your world shook

And I love how you look

When we talk on video phone

Hearing your voice of perfect tone

So I would love to meet

Which for me would be treat

Making me blissful like long ago

When I was in divine flow

But now I go to church

As through the years I search

The world for an ideal Bride

From whom I cannot truly hide

Depths of my amour and devotion

Filling my soul like an ocean.

8/06/33-25:DEW0057—07/09/18

Considering Future Coaching About Schizophrenia

It's not my fault I'm ill

But many people stigmatize me still

Even though I take my meds

And have not seen hospital beds

For more than twenty-five years

So it's not one of the fears

That used to cause me tears

But I have learned to forgive

Those who in ignorance Dew live

And condemn the image of stereotype

I'd like from world to wipe

Since condition does cause much pain

As afflicted strive to be sane

And overcome all that they suffer

Even when their struggle gets tougher

For world I'd like to illuminate

About sickness created by random Fate

That leaves many victims madly bawling

Which is why I got calling

To speak about disease in truth

That most contracted during innocent youth.

8/07/33-25:DEW0058—07/10/18

When Love Transforms Into Hate

When a person is extremely lonely

They think of one thing only

Which is how to beat solitude

So they take on yearning attitude

Making them into a needy dude

Willing to Dew anything for lover

They can entice under blanket's cover

Of bed where the nightly sleep

Slipping into an amorous dream deep

Until the night they have sex

Which does the relationship often hex

As both experience change of emotion

Unless they've been given magic potion

Keeping the affaire full of bliss

Getting more intense with every kiss

But sometimes the exact opposite occurs

Where pussy hisses instead of purrs

And devotion turns into vicious fight

From which both parties take flight

For this is how passion goes

As from cherished ashes frustration grows.

A Prayer For Friday Morn

I just want to thank God

For use of this Earthly bod

The Deity Who is eternally real

And knows always how I feel

Loving me when I was sick

And tried my shrink to trick

Into thinking I was not schizophrenic

Which I wasn't able to Dew

As before my eyes life flew

While praising You for beautiful females

With whom I drank many ales

That led to multiple sweet kisses

But ultimately never to a missus

Who would be with me forever

In deep relationship nothing could sever

Though women have been Best Friends

To You Lord my soul sends

The truest words of pure devotion

In my moments of concrete emotion

Pondering sacrifice of Your only Son

Who against death and devil won.

8/09/33-25:DEW0060—07/12/18

Quandary That's Driving Me Nuts

Will I ever again make love

To feel ecstasy of Velvet Glove

Discovered more than forty years ago

Since which I have flown solo

And turned from intense to mellow

Composing verse alone in this place

Exploring vastness of my inner space

Externally waiting for the starship Dialina

Hearing recently from beautiful lady Nina

Whom I knew as nubile girl

As precious as finest black pearl

Who is back in my sphere

Though she does not live near

Having settled on the West Coast

But she stimulates my libido most

Dew to radiance of her smile

Wanting deeply her number to dial

But she insists on calling me

Because she desires to be free

From obligations her form does allow

So I'm awaiting her contact now.

8/10/33-25:DEW0061—07/13/18

A Truly Bird-Brained Contemplation

Seven crows landed on two trees

Unaware of the hot summer breeze

And pondered the state of Earth

Which they felt had lost worth

In every age of human history

Philosophizing on depths of Lord's mystery

Sending Jesus to create sacred peace

Which only caused violence to increase

As tribes pursued religion with zeal

Since not one is exclusively real

For all people who inspired feel

Until their chatter turned to Duck

The bird in human body stuck

"Two score and three years ago

He became 'schizophrenic' going with Flow

And was put in mental unit

Though he is the Holy Spirit

Trying to prove humanity is insane

Until he actually imploded his brain

Which made him into 'Supreme Quack'

Invulnerable to any type of attack."

8/11/33-25:DEW0062—07/14/18

Dear Ones Who Are Gone

My first friend died in fire

Having on my psyche effect dire

And next went goalie pal Wayne

Whose demise almost drove me insane

So great was my mental pain

Then Shane was killed on bike

Dewing what he most did like

And many were murderedby cancer

Including Kayron the singer and dancer

As well as the famous Remo

Who did to lung disease did go

Not to mention greatest buddy Chuck

Who fell to attack by muck

While I mourn the incomparable Randi

Her love was sweet as candy

And most recently butts doomed Bri

Unable about quitting smokes to lies

Like my most beloved mother Mary

Teaching me true love to carry

Married to the truly honorable Judge

Who never did from integrity budge.

8/12/33-25:DEW0063—07/15/18

Brief Resume Of Ultimate Muse

She's a southern belle in Savannah

Not to be confused with Havana

Though both are near the ocean

And she causes me deep emotion

Especially when I consider her heart

Which is inspiration for my art

Since I'd like Romance to start

Where we'd hold each other tight

Through the dark and Apocalyptic night

When Christ will return to Earth

And all discover reason for birth

Being either a sheep or goat

Who will not be aboard boat

Bound for Heaven of God's house

But none will have a spouse

For that is a worldly concept

Unknown where everyone is an adept

At mastering the skills of amour

And nobody is ever a bore

As great Lord we eternally glorify

For making sure we don't die.

8/13/33-25:DEW0064—07/16/18

A Thousand Years From Now

They say I was Enlightened One

Who knew how to have fun

And I was a pretty boy

Bringing to girls a sublime joy

In youth by being sexual toy

Which caused many females to smile

Whom I entertained for brief while

But mine wasn't easy existence

For I dealt with mental disease

That put my brain on fire

So no offspring could I sire

Since I was in fact insane

And suffered inordinate amount of pain

Perhaps because I declared myself divine

And appropriated Lord's throne as mine

For which I paid the price

Even while pursuing life of vice

Being torn between doubt and bliss

And never finding my perfect miss

Whom I could call my Bride

To have eternally at my side.

8/14/33-25:DEW0065—07/17/18

Wandering The Streets In Summer

There's a plethora of beauties today

In this city where I stay

And I love all feminine forms

Like coeds in the university dorms

Who entice young men to lust

With sweet curves of precocious bust

Into whose eyes I did gaze

While their smiles did me amaze

As I moved through adolescent phase

When all I wanted was wet kiss

In order to reach Romantic bliss

Until I moved into adult life

And fell into deep mental strife

So I lost my playboy appeal

Which did my charisma cruelly steal

With the result I never married

As stigma of illness I carried

Which destroyed all my amorous illusions

Becoming lost in inescapable divine delusions

Through now I am very happy

Despite fact I'll never be pappy.

8/15/33-25:DEW0066—07/18/18

She Is Still Queen Muse

I've a Best Female Friend Elizabeth

Whom I will love until death

And shares name with my sis

Who as child caused me bliss

And now is mother of two

Young men to themselves always true

Proud to be nephews of DEW

Who cannot turn back on Muse

Happy with man she did choose

Though I tried hard to romance

Her when I had the chance

But amorous stars did not align

Perhaps because I drank no wine

But still I cherish her so

While still our friendship does grow

With each year getting more close

Continuing to ingest a stronger dose

Of devotion that we cannot share

Despite fact we make perfect pair

But I'm doomed to be alone

Satisfied with her voice on phone.

8/16/33-25:DEW0067—07/19/18

I Still Yearn For Her

She was prototype for Velvet Velour

Who reached me to my core

But another man she did marry

So feelings I had to bury

Now being mother to two girls

As precious as thousand large pearls

While I loved her scarlet hair

And her body curvaceous and fair

At which other men did stare

With fingers both long and frail

As about her I wrote tale

That will echo through many years

Which produced laughter leading to tears

A modern myth from my heart

In which she played critical part

But still I love her so

More than anyone can ever know

Including women whom I have adored

Though with them I never soared

To heights of an eagle summit

She created with her beauteous wit.

The Greater Of My Inspirations

I would rather be women seducing

Than a plethora of poems producing

For although verse is my passion

I'm turned on by female fashion

As they and the weather grow hot

But I feel like a robot

Since taking last toke of pot

More than a long decade ago

Causing my sex life to slow

Now longer craving primo Colombian gold

Which in legal shops isn't sold

But all I desire is kiss

To guarantee my elusive marital bliss

With the lady of eternal yearning

As about eternity I am learning

Because I write like a machine

Trying to create portrait of Queen

I fear I'll not find here

On Earth in the future near

But I have loved my life

That with struggles has been rife.

8/18/33-25:DEW0069—07/21/18

In Order To Answer Calling

I want to learn to coach

In a field few dare broach

In which I have much experience

That has made strong my presence

Wanting to talk to loved ones

Such as parents who have sons

And daughters who became mentally ill

Who must take an antipsychotic pill

To keep their inner demons still

Trying to maintain a fragile sanity

Which compromises self esteem and vanity

So I want to help fight

For vision they've lost in night

Since brains are out of whack

So they're convinced world does attack

Their perceptions senses and emotions

To reveal there is no magic potion

To help win the battles hard

Like writing Poetry equal to Bard

In war that lasts a lifetime

Attempting to give reason behind rhyme.

8/19/33-25:DEW0070—07/22/18

Birthday Of Best Female Friend

Because you are indeed so beautiful

You need a lover who's dutiful

And will respect all your wishes

Which is not to wash dishes

For you've desire for something great

A quotidian life will not sate

Since yours is a unique Fate

Knowing the radiance of your heart

Which is inspiration for my art

And why you remain "Queen Muse"

Despite fact you did not choose

To make me your only man

But still I am your biggest fan

As it's you I unconditionally adore

Wanting to waltz across ballroom floor

Holding you in my devoted arms

So hot they set off alarms

While I fantasize about deep embrace

That will implode time and space

Which I know is a dream

Forever ecstatic you're on my team.

8/22/33-25:DEW0073—07/25/18

Birthday Wishes For Ultimate Muse

Though we haven't know each other

Long I realize you're a awesome mother

And fact we met by chance

Leads me to thoughts of Romance

As we execute twin flame dance

Which may just be an illusion

In my mind full of confusion

But I find you very attractive

Since to stimuli I am reactive

And I wish you great day

As new year gets under way

Orbiting again around the illuminated sun

Hoping your time's full of fun

For I crave time to meet

So to walk together down street

Of fulfilled dreams we both share

Because for you I truly care

And admire the way you persevere

Through adversity in now and here

Having survived pain of broken wing

While of you I poetically sing.

8/22/33-25:DEW0073—08/25/18

Day Both Happy And Sad

One year ago Father Roger died

Unable from Grim Reaper to hide

And he was a fantastic man

Looking after family best he can

Leaving behind three daughters and wife

Me only son in his life

But now he's in God's embrace

No longer part of human race

But he was not my Dad

Who loved me through periods mad

For that distinction goes to The Judge

Who through my psychosis didn't budge

Always giving me love and support

Against insanity I treated as sport

But today is also the anniversary

Of two women I would marry

If either gave me the chance

To show essence of pure Romance

For they are two principal Muses

Whom my poetic verse always amuses

But neither for paramour me chooses.

8/22/33-25:DEW0073—07/25/18

How Dew I Tell Her?

There are some things plainly tragic

That cannot be fixed by magic

And this is such a case

I truly don't want to face

But I alone to Queen Muse

Must be bearer of bad news

Which will make her composure lose

As for months she hasn't cried

But her dear Kieran has died

And I must tell her the Truth

Though he was a relative youth

Not wanting to break her heart

I must use skill of Art

To soften blow of his demise

But I see in her eyes

The pain this knowledge will cause

Despite the power of Earthly laws

That decree mortality is a fact

Which never arrives with any tact

As we all return to dust

So in God we must trust.

8/23/33-25:DEW0074—07/26/18

Being Rather Hard On Reality

Forty three years I've been sick

Making life seem like surreal flick

But I've tried not to complain

When staying rational was a strain

And I never found compatible mate

But perhaps it's not too late

Though most women are like jailbait

As Jill who did herself in

Thereby committing the great mortal sin

Which is to kill your soul

Leaving in Universe a vast hole

Of an inescapable and eternal despair

With her life I couldn't share

While she spends forever in hell

Like our first parents who fell

From an ideal existence in Paradise

With absolutely no concept of vice

Until they both ate forbidden fruit

As devil encouraged false divine pursuit

And so I exist and suffer

Even though each day is tougher.

8/25/33-25:DEW0076—07/28/18

Essence Of The Human Condition

No one can ultimately escape death

As all must take final breath

Whether one is young or old

Their entire story must be told

As time inexorably continues to unfold

And though this fact causes sadness

It doesn't prevent sense of gladness

That we have years on Earth

From the moment of traumatic birth

Which allows us joyfully to play

Endlessly in a truly youthful way

As we cherish father and mother

While being conscientious sister or brother

To siblings with whom we grow

And lovers we get to know

With whom we can create offspring

After exchanging a precious golden ring

That lets us forget the tragic

And enjoy brief but intense magic

Of amour that can blossom forever

Finding in love a diversion clever.

A World Full Of Women

I have seen fine female forms

Many of whom lived in dorms

When I was an ambitious student

Who always said what I meant

Though being insane at the time

And thinking sex was a crime

Which would put me in hell

Even if Truth I did tell

Believing I could my soul sell

In order to get forever high

Never considering that I must die

Until the day I actually did

When neutrons blew off my lid

Leaving body to rot in Hackensack

Convinced I'd never make it back

To experience life again on Earth

But God gave me new birth

To find here my sole amour

Whom I'd love to the core

Up to the end of Eternity

When I finally achieve belated paternity.

8/28/33-25:DEW0079—07/31/18

The Sirenic Nymph Of Hackensack

Her smile has a great beauty

Lovely as pass from Doug Flutie

And her eyes illuminate the bar

Sparkling to those near and far

With chassis classic as any car

While enthusiasm I contain just barely

Because I see her so rarely

But she is mere fantasy

About whom to dream is easy

But to me she's as a child

Making my desire for her mild

As we only very recently met

Both of us caught in net

Of permanent residents of this town

On whose head I place crown

As she pursues a psychological degree

To become private therapist for me

Making me feel an adolescent infatuation

Wanting with her to take vacation

To Garden of the Lord's Paradise

Where I could kiss her twice.

8/29/33-25:DEW0080—08/01/18

Dewing Well For Sixty-Three

I still love rock and roll

And listen to old Motown soul

Living forty years in this room

From whence I never became bridegroom

And I am "World's Greatest Poet"

As every night I compose verse

In order to neutralize my curse

Thanking the Lord for my talent

I did not inherit from parent

Hoping to regain Garden of Eden

Though I Dew not know when

Or who will be my Eve

But from Earth I will leave

Despite fact I've sired no offspring

About whom in rhyme to sing

But I have known many beauties

I ignored because of my duties

To mollify the effects of Apocalypse

Which began with timely lunar eclipse

That began on my twentieth birthday

And still is having its way.

8/30/33-25:DEW0081—08/02/18

Confessions Of A Permanent Bachelor

There is something wrong with me

I've gone through life wife-free

And never took that decisive step

That stopped me from being Prep

To escape my high-school days

And leave behind my adolescent ways

As I feel into schizophrenic haze

So I never met right female

Who'd accept thought God is Dale

Sentenced to hell for thirty years

About which were shed many tears

By women whom I did love

Who let me wear Velvet Glove

As with them I adored sex

While breaking up did me vex

But I did not become grouch

Making out on my dilapidated couch

In apartment where I still live

Lord with benevolence did me give

To await advent of His Son

And I have had great fun.

8/31/33-25:DEW0082—08/03/18

Delusions Are Never Totally Eliminated

Given how much I did toke

It's miracle I gave up smoke

And all the other illegal drugs

Including my endless consumption of mugs

Of beer I imbibed for decades

Having enthusiastic sex with gorgeous maids

And I say in language plain

I am Lord of my domain

Here at home of the sane

Which is the City of Stars

With its fair share of bars

Where I drink soda and cranberry

As drunken loads I don't carry

So better to scope lovely dames

Rarely discovering what are their names

But still at them I smile

And female friends I constantly dial

To be enchanted by sirenic voices

Smooth as engines of Rolls-Royces

Rolling over sacred streets of gold

Where angels reside I am told.

Back To Being A Bachelor

I think I have lost Sher

She whom I often call "Chere"

Because I thought her Ultimate Muse

But now she's vanished without clues

Which I don't know for fact

Not knowing how she will act

Since I've known her but short while

But I treasure her laughing smile

That I have seen of Skype

When she gave me no hype

And I saw she's my type

As I pray her mother's well

Who in her own house fell

And was in hospital two weeks

So now again health she seeks

In rehab where she's lost weight

While she tries slowly to recuperate

But perhaps I am being dramatic

Since our conversations were not automatic

Though she is Being of Spirit

For my Romantic lamp she lit.

8/33/33-25:DEW0084—08/05/18

Another Work Inspired By Illness

I am truly talented Poetic artist

Who writes with a schizophrenic twist

Which is load I have carried

That kept me from getting married

Putting me in Hospital fifteen times

Though I never committed any crimes

Medicating myself with many absurd rhymes

While blessed with deeply loving parents

Responsible for a few voluntary commitments

That were initiated by my shrink

Slipping into psychosis in a blink

From which medications did save me

So that now I am free

To spend my days in room

Where I'll stay until Apocalyptic doom

When Jesus will return to Earth

And all shall experience second birth

Unless they are condemned to hell

Like angels who from Heaven fell

Into Pandemonium in time long ago

As countless sacred generations will grow.

8/34/33-25:DEW0085—08/06/18

Still Great Despite My Diagnosis

I have had lots of luck

Not in Hospital to be stuck

Always supported by my best friends

Although often showing some irrational trends

And my family has been great

To save me from psychotic state

When I did not take medications

Making it obvious by all indications

That I'd temporarily lost my mind

As I left normal world behind

In order to true self find

But now I am in remission

Able to relate my artistic vision

Living a life free of stress

For forty years at same address

Protected by my verse and books

No longer disturbed by strange looks

From people ignorant of my condition

While I pursue my Poetic ambition

Producing works just about every night

Trying into darkness to bring light.

8/35/33-25:DEW0086—08/07/18

Reflection Of A Provisional Immortal

I don't worry about dying tomorrow

Which would cause world great sorrow

Because I trust in the Lord

With Whom I have an accord

That if I stay completely straight

I can decide my own Fate

To live unspecified amount of years

Even as others shed many tears

And of death have great fears

While I live inspired every day

As in my Poetry I say

Loudly my gratitude for this life

Although it's been filled with strife

That's been overcome by expansive amour

Vast as ocean on a shore

Made up of perfect black sand

Where I'll make my final stand

Against the enemy with no name

Trying to fill me with shame

For mistakes I made in past

Which were sins that didn't last.

The Pooch Of Queen Muse

She has a big black dog

In her life a critical cog

Who was with her through hurricanes

And when she suffered withdrawal pains

Caused by meds prescribed by shrink

Who was quack and didn't think

Of dangers of extremely high dose

That put her to death close

Which is not what she chose

In order to overcome her condition

From which she suffered in addition

To solitude to which she's prone

So that she was often alone

If not for her canine "son"

Who is truly the only one

Loving her with his noble heart

Since from her he wouldn't depart

No matter how badly she felt

Content with hand he was dealt

And she returned love in kind

Being to his animal limitations blind.

8/37/33-25:DEW0088—08/09/18

The Easy Consolation Of Romance

Ultimate Muse gave me a call

Making me feel ten feet tall

And I could sense her smile

Telling jokes across many a mile

While I started truly to rejoice

When I heard her soft voice

Always for my lonely psyche great

Even if she's not my mate

I can hold in an embrace

For hours kissing her lovely face

Absorbing beauty of her in lace

But still I cherish her friendship

And might well take long trip

To finally meet this Southern belle

About whom in Poetry I tell

The secrets of all my desires

Which cause in my heart fires

Of longing burning out of control

As I try to trade soul

For a passion that will last

With woman who is sensual blast.

8/38/33-25:DEW0089—08/10/18

Dreaming Of The Ideal One

I want to hold your hand

And lie with you in sand

Of some idyllic tropical isle beach

To the other Romance to teach

Holding you in arms of amour

While waves wash across the shore

As we enthusiastically engage in embrace

Lost in reveries of deep space

Where every star shines sun bright

And we bask in the light

Driving away darkness of endless night

Trusting in the Lord to provide

Love from which we cannot hide

Passing our time on sweet Earth

Caught between both tragedy and mirth

We experience with every passing year

Alternating between laughter and a tear

As we watch loved ones die

So often we don't even cry

But rather have faith in God

As on the planet we've trod

Pondering reality of all possible trips

While praying we shall survive Apocalypse.

8/39/33-25:DEW0090—08/11/18

Metaphysical Reflection On Monday Night

The Holy Spirit is the Source

Of what is proper human course

Going straight neither left nor right

Always keeping God's will in sight

Secure in knowledge of His Grace

Wanting forever to view the face

Of Lord who died on cross

Which to Earth was eternal loss

Until He rose to become Boss

Whose blood was shed for mankind

Who could never again Paradise find

For which every person does search

Whether or not they attend church

For humanity wants to experience bliss

Which is gift they always miss

Seeking to create salvation with money

Or some other idol that's funny

To the saint who discovers wisdom

By following the path to Kingdom

Jesus revealed when he did preach

So finally Heavenly Throne to reach.

Trying To Be Muse Worthy

Right now I'm not the me

That I truly want to be

Living alone in this messy pad

I have inhabited since being lad

When I finished with shrink's Program

Making me the person I am

Poor as they say Poets are

Without a house or a car

Looking for my unique Romantic star

I don't know I'll ever find

Though to everybody I am kind

As I pass life in Hackensack

To where I always come back

And I have loved countless beauties

While I never forgot my duties

To represent the Lord on Earth

The mission I've pursued since birth

Even when I was party boy

Who was a famous girl toy

Until the well did run dry

And I finally stopped getting high.

9/01/33-25:DEW0091—08/13/18

Diana Is On The Dialina

You are my only Latina Princess

Your presence does the world bless

Beautiful as the sky at night

When all stars show their light

But it's your Spirit I adore

Being Reality which I live for

Though I am just Poet poor

Trying to paint a verbal masterpiece

As you care for precious niece

For you fill me with hope

Since with difficulties I daily cope

Living in our quiet common hometown

Where you display your royal crown

And drive speedily in your car

Even though you don't patronize bar

Where I no longer drink beer

Wanting only you to be near

So we can find bliss together

No matter how stormy the weather

Because over my heart you reign

Never feeling with you any pain.

9/01/33-25:DEW0091—08/13/18

Truthful To Myself And Others

Many people say I am courageous

Because I have an illness outrageous

Only coping with hand I'm dealt

While accepting the death of Svelte

Who was love of my life

I wanted to make my wife

But that obviously will not occur

Despite fact she was divinely pure

Though now gone for thirty years

I miss more as mortality nears

While trying to keep happy face

In Holiest City that's my base

Where I've spent entire adult existence

Which has been quite an experience

Getting to know many dear friends

As I went through fashionable trends

Of drugs I shouldn't have done

Although they were lots of fun

And I truly have few regrets

Having won most of my bets.

Every Day Is A Blessing

If by chance I die tonight

I will face it without fear

For I've had truly wonderful life

Though it's been fraught with strife

And I wish I'd found Bride

To be always by my side

Who didn't from my devotion hide

While igniting my heart with fire

Filling my Spirit with unquenchable desire

So I could have had offspring

Who would have made Angels sing

But I was truly mentally ill

As every morning I need pill

To keep away the intense pain

Of brain that many considered insane

Though Reality could have been worse

For I consoled myself writing verse

That helped many people have revelation

Of state of my psychotic situation

And if it's not my time

I'll continue to create unpredictable rhyme.

9/04/33-25:DEW0094-08/16/18

A Roxette To Ultimate Muse

I don't remember the exact date

We were brought together by Fate

But it was Destiny we'd meet

And become to each other sweet

But I thank Lord for serendipity

Though you weren't in my city

But still our encounter has validity

In my quest to find Romance

As my joy you dew enhance

Though a thousand miles from me

In truth longing to you see

As your sensual voice does remind

Me of what treasure I find

In simple act of knowing you

Whose heart is pure and true

And who is full of knowledge

That transports me to the edge

Of secret arts I don't know

As with Poetry I Dew show

The true depths of my devotion

While I swim across love's ocean.

9/06/33-25:DEW0096—08/18/18

Another Muse On The Horizon

I think about my Belle Michelle

For whom long ago I fell

With her bright smile and tattoos

Who sometimes gets the mortal blues

When friends move to next plane

And causes her a great pain

Which from her does energy drain

But still she creates strong front

Realizing death isn't a clever stunt

People in jest do thoughtlessly perform

Always leading to an emotional storm

Though the loved ones still survive

Tragically sad they dew remain alive

When their beloveds ascend on high

Not even aware they did die

Which she feels more than most

Giving to their memory heartfelt toast

To memorialize their life of joy

They experienced since being a boy

And I admire her deep grief

Although time on Earth is brief.

9/07/33-25:DEW0097—08/19/18

In Admiration Of Ultimate Muse

I thought I knew a lot

But on you I've got nothing

As you're maestra of esoteric arts

You're broken down into many parts

And I'm blown away by knowledge

You have pulling me to ledge

Of the ever expanding great unknown

That you have already me shown

I imagined only while smoking bone

I did often in my youth

While diligently pursuing an intoxicated truth

But you understand crystals and cards

Going back to time of bards

While also having read endless books

That few have given serious looks

And yet you are incredibly attractive

As with yoga you remain active

For of Angel you remind me

In your defense of thought free

Even as I ponder your soul

Transformed into diamond from common coal.

9/08/33-25:DEW0098—08/20/18

When The Time Is Right

Whoever falls in love with Poetry

I write is woman for me

And I might well be alone

Talking to females only by phone

But I'll be the person I am

Not accepting passion that's a sham

For I'll never be a scam

Having been taught by my mother

That people should respect one another

And of my work I'm proud

Especially when I read it aloud

Although editors dew not accept it

Despite my obvious intelligence and wit

And my skill at composing verse

Which always gets better never worse

But I want to touch heart

Of one lady with this art

To which I've dedicated my life

Trying to find my perfect wife

Who will adore words I choose

For I've definitely paid my dues.

9/10/33-25:DEW0100—08/22/18

I'm In Love With You

I imagine that you and me

Are in a field completely free

To laugh to play to love

In harmony with the Lord above

And this I've wanted to say

To you from the first day

Inspired Fate brought us into contact

And I saw what I'd lacked

Through all the years of solitude

When I had major chauvinistic attitude

And with lust all women viewed

Having sex with no real devotion

Hoping to discover secret passion potion

Happy that I had no Bride

Making me see you on side

While distracting my longing for you

To whom I'll always be true

For I know you're chosen amour

Causing my Spirit forever to soar

To Jesus on His Heavenly Throne

As into deep agape I've grown.

9/11/33-25:DEW0101—08/23/18

Birthday Tribute To Beloved Sibling

You are my real big Sis

Who happily has found marital bliss

For which I Dew congratulate you

As you celebrate every day anew

And we've experienced a lot together

With mother as unpredictable as weather

But life's been to us fine

While the sun still does shine

In the towns that we love

Though in winter we require glove

To shield us from snow above

And I truly cherish your presence

For of amour you are essence

As another orbit comes and goes

When from forest fires smoke blows

But you are safe with Frank

For whom nightly Lord I thank

And I pray that new year

Will bring you joy and cheer

As we live united by birth

Hoping Jesus will save the Earth.

9/12/33-25:DEW0102—08/24/18

This Should Be Labor Day

Today is the day between birthdays

Of two sisters gone different ways

Though both are very happily married

And the younger two boys carried

Nine months in womb to birth

Whose presences have blessed the Earth

Filling it with their integrity's worth

And I love them very dearly

Especially now that I see clearly

The reciprocation that they give me

For the person who is free

To live existence no longer ill

As long as I take pill

Four times a day to regulate

Cranial chemical imbalance that's my Fate

Wishing I could create real communication

That would fix their fractured relation

But I refuse to take sides

In chaos of their rollercoaster rides

On which they seem deeply stuck

Contrary to the philosophy of Duck.

9/13/33-25:DEW0103—08/25/18

www.ingramcontent.com/pod-product-compliance
Lightning Source LLC
Chambersburg PA
CBHW080457030726
47592CB00011B/3152

9 781798 051078